TOM AND TILLY'S CHRISTMAS PLAY

Helen and Hilton Thomas

Tom and Tilly's Christmas Play

© Helen and Hilton Thomas 2017.

The moral rights of the authors have been asserted.

All rights reserved. Except as permitted under the *Australian Copyright Act* 1968 (for example, fair dealing for the purposes of study, research, criticism or review), no part of this book may be reproduced, stored in a retrieval system, communicated, or transmitted in any form or by any means without prior written permission. All enquiries should be made to the Helen Thomas. helen.thomas@wise.works.

First published 2017

Publisher: Grubooks

Email: orders@grubooks.com

ISBN: 9781925319095 (paperback)

ISBN 9781925319101 (Epub)

Children's' Fiction.
Christmas
Animals; Sheep.

Tom and Tilly's Christmas Play

It was early morning. The sun was about to rise. Bud and Josie, the parents of Tom and Tilly, were waking up from a deep sleep. "Let's try and not make a noise, it would be nice to have Tom and Tilly sleeping a bit longer." So, Bud and Josie very quietly tip-toed into the garden.

They had a breakfast of fresh grass and maize, with a drink of water.

"Yum", said Josie that tasted so good. Bud and Josie were having a little quiet time before their two babies woke up. It wasn't too long after that when Tom and Tilly woke up. "Good morning Mummy," said Tilly, "Oh where are they? Perhaps they are outside having breakfast." Tilly was right. She ran over to their Mum and Dad.

"Hello my Darlings, did you both have a good night?" asked Josie.

"Yes, thank you," said Tom.

"Now come over to me and have your breakfast." Which they did, and enjoyed it.

It was the season of Christmas, and the local Church was looking for real live animals to use for the Crib which was going to be held outdoors, in the Church grounds. The lambs' owners, Chris and Barb, and their two children, Sarah and Sam, who were twins, were really so excited at the thought of their lambs being able to take part in the Nativity play, that they had to tell their family and friends.

Tom and Tilly's Christmas Play

Sarah and Sam ran over to the lambs and started telling them the exciting news. "Guess what Tom and Tilly, we have been asked to bring you both and your Mummy and Daddy to the local Nativity play as they wish to have live animals. The Vicar would like to have a newborn baby, to place in the crib, too. Mrs Sinclair has just had her baby boy. The Vicar is going over tonight after dinner to ask Mr and Mrs Sinclair if they can let them have their new baby son to play the part of the Baby Jesus."

They drive to the Sinclair's House and ring the doorbell, "Hello and welcome, do come in" said Bob, "Vicki!" he called out to his wife, "Chris and Barb and the children have arrived."

"I'll be down in a few minutes. Just changing Josh's nappy."

Vicki came into the room with baby Josh, "isn't he gorgeous," said Barb.

Just then, the doorbell rang again. It was Scott Smith, the vicar. "Come in, Scott," said Bob. "Chris and Bob are here with their children."

"Excellent," Scott replied, "I wanted to talk about who would be in the Nativity play. We need to get it organised and start rehearsing soon."

They sat down in the living room and Scott said "I always like to have a real baby for the baby Jesus. Could we borrow Josh?"

"Certainly," said Vikki, "I would really like my baby to be baby Jesus. It would be lovely."

The vicar opened a pad with notes about the play. "We need the rest of the cast."

"Would Sarah and Sam like to play Mary and Joseph?" suggested Vikki.

"Yes! Please!" the twins shouted at the same time.

Tom and Tilly's Christmas Play

"That's great," said Scott. "Now, I must go, as I have to phone some other families and find people for the other parts. I was thinking of Peter Lee for the innkeeper, William and Harry Thomas for shepherds, and David Harris, Francis Day, and John Green as the three wise men.

"Would three o'clock on Wednesday be OK for the first rehearsal?"

"That's fine." said Chris "How about having our lambs, Tom and Tilly? Sorry, I can't offer a donkey, or cows and horses."

The vicar said that he had models for the donkey, cows and a horse, from last year but he would love to have real lambs.

The vicar was very pleased that the rest of the parents had given their permission for their children to take part in the Christmas play.

Everyone was so excited about being in the play and about the rehearsal. The twins could hardly sleep, with excitement. But they woke up early on Wednesday and went to talk to their lambs, Tom and Tilly.

"Hey, lambs," Sam shouted as soon as they were in the field. Of course, all the sheep ran away when he shouted, but then Tom looked round to see what all the commotion was about. He saw it was only Sam and Sarah, so he galloped back across the field and rubbed his nose against Sarah's side. Sarah rubbed his back, which he loved, and stroked his head. Sam was, by then cuddling Tilly and getting barged by Bud, the lambs' dad.

More quietly, but still very excited, Sam said "The vicar said yesterday that you can be in the play. The first rehearsal is Wednesday afternoon. You will have to be very good and not run away."

Sam and Sarah's dad came by and told them that the lambs could not go to the rehearsal. "The rehearsal will be in the village hall so definitely no sheep or lambs." He said. "They will have to wait until the day, or perhaps the dress rehearsal, that's the last practice, may be outside."

After lunch, Sarah's Mum found a blue smock and altered it to fit Sarah.

It was Wednesday morning. Sarah awoke with a start. "Today is the rehearsal," she thought. It was still dark, so she knew she was not allowed to get up. She tried to go back to sleep but she was so excited, she could not sleep.

After ages, there was a little light outside the window. Sarah looked at her watch. It was five o'clock. That meant she could get up. Very quietly she crept over to Sam and woke him.

"It's the rehearsal today!" Sarah said, "Get up!"

"Not for ages," said Sam. "I want to sleep some more."

Sarah put on her clothes and ran outside to the field where the lambs were. "Tom and Tilly, It's the rehearsal today!" Tom and

Tilly went on munching grass and maize. "Silly sheep – why don't you understand?" Sarah asked them. The lambs looked up and then went back to their munching.

❧

Brrring! The bell sounded for the end of school. Sarah jumped up, grabbed Sam's arm and dragged him across the playground to the area they had to wait for their parents to pick them up.

"Hey! What's all the hurry?" Sam asked.

"Remember! It's the play rehearsal. Mum will be here soon to take us"

"Oh, yes," Sam remembered he had to practice playing Joseph. "I suppose we have to."

"Come on!" Said Sarah. "It will be fun."

Soon their Mum arrived and they were on their way to the hall.

Mrs Smith, the Vicar's wife, welcomed them at the hall. "Have you got any costumes?" She asked.

Sarah showed her the blue smock. Mrs Smith thought it was perfect. She had some clothes for Joseph. Sam tried them on and they fitted him well.

She handed out clothes to the other children. Then she gave everyone a piece of material like a tea towel. Sarah's had pale blue stripes along the edges.

"What do we do with these?" Sarah asked.

"Israel is a hot country. The people wore these on their heads to protect them from the sun." and Mrs Smith showed them how to tie them. They all looked at themselves in the mirrors. Now they looked quite different and more grown-up in their clothes.

The Vicar arrived carrying a bundle of scripts. He handed one to each child. "Your parts are all highlighted." He said, "Make sure you learn your own part. You have to know it absolutely, and learn the last words the previous person says so you know when to start talking. By the dress rehearsal, you need to be quite sure of your own parts and not need the books. I am sure your parents will help you learn."

"Now, I want to go through the whole play." The Vicar continued. "I am reading the Narrator's part. We will not do the actions this time, just sit around and read."

They all sat on the chairs in a circle and the Vicar started to read "Long ago, in a place called Nazareth …" he started.

Sarah and Sam were listening intently and then Mrs Smith said, "Read your part, Sam."

Sam quickly found the part in his book and read "Hello Innkeeper, is there a room in the Inn, My wife is going to have a baby soon and we are very tired."

Then Peter answered, as the Innkeeper, and the children and the Vicar read through the rest of the play.

"That was very good." Said the Vicar. "Now read your lines over and over and really learn them well. Don't forget to learn where you come in as well. At the next rehearsal on Friday, we will try it with you doing all the actions."

"Can we bring the lambs?" Sarah asked.

"Not until the dress rehearsal on Sunday morning." The Vicar replied, "We can't have them in the hall, can we?"

When Sarah saw the hall on Friday she couldn't believe the change. Screens had been arranged to make it look like a room.

"I hope you all know your lines." The Vicar said.

The children all shouted "Yes." They had been practising hard to learn their parts in the play.

"Sarah and Sam stand here." Said the Vicar. "You will walk up to the inn door, in the rehearsal but when we do the play Mary (Sarah) will be on the donkey and Joseph, (Sam) will pull it along."

"Peter. You are the Innkeeper. Go behind that screen on the right and stay there until Joseph knocks. Let's try the first scene."

The Vicar read the introduction then the twins walked up to the screen where Peter was, and Sam knocked, hard, on it.

Crash! Bang! Ouch! The screen fell over knocking Peter onto the floor.

"Try it again, but a more gentle knock this time." Said the Vicar when all the scenery had been put back in place and Peter realised he was not really hurt.

This time it went just as it was meant to. Sam asked Peter if there was any room and Peter said all the rooms were taken, but when he understood Mary was pregnant, he said there was a stable and Joseph and Mary could stay there with the animals.

In the next scene, Sarah and Sam were in the stable. Sarah was sitting on a chair and Sam was putting the doll representing baby Jesus on another chair for the manger. They could not have Josh, the real baby, until the actual performance on Sunday.

On Saturday Sarah, Sam, and their Mum and Dad went to the see the Sinclairs. Vikki wanted Sarah to practice holding the baby. First Sarah had to sit down and Vikki showed her how to cradle Josh in her arms. She had to hold one arm supporting his body and support his head with her hand. Vikki was worried that in the excitement of the play Sarah would forget and hurt the baby, but Sarah showed she could hold him properly.

Sam wanted to hold Josh as well and in the rehearsal, he had put the doll in the manger. So he too sat down and practised holding the baby. Soon they could both show they could be trusted with Josh.

Sarah was, again, first up on Sunday. First, she went out and gave the lambs a special cuddle because they had so much to do today. Then she carefully cleaned them up so they would be really smart for the play.

After breakfast, the twins helped their Dad load fencing and poles into the ute and take them to the field outside the hall. Dad put up the fence to make an enclosure and filled a water trough in it.

The Vicar and some other parents were putting up scenery, and putting chairs out on the grass.

Then the twins and their Dad went and fetched the lambs, Tom and Tilly, and the sheep, Bud and Josie. They put them in the pen they had made and let them drink the water and eat some hay.

At ten, they all arrived back at the field: The Twins, Mum and Dad, Bob and Vikki with Josh. The Vicar and Mrs Smith were already there with the other children who were going to be in the play.

Tom and Tilly's Christmas Play

Sarah and Sam's Dad showed the children who were going to be shepherds, how to handle the lambs. They were very excited about this and Mrs Smith had to tell them, over and over, to calm down.

The scenery had been finished and the children were all dressed up for the play. Sarah had a pillow inside her smock so she looked pregnant. She was very proud of how she looked and showed off her 'baby-bump' to everyone.

The Vicar now called everyone together for the rehearsal and said a prayer. They had to kneel on the ground and be very quiet during this.

Mrs Smith looked after the cast members until they were needed for the play. She had to stop the boys trying to take the lambs out too early.

The Vicar started to read the play and then Sarah climbed on to the donkey (which had big bicycle wheels on each side). Sam started to walk towards the Inn, pulling the donkey.

It was difficult to steer the donkey and Sam had to go round and push it to get it in the right direction. He said "Silly Neddy, Why won't you go straight?" Everybody laughed.

The Vicar said "Very funny Sam, but try to stick to the script, please"

Sam pulled the donkey, with Sarah, up to the door and knocked loudly with his staff. This time the door did not collapse. It just opened and Peter came out.

The curtain was pulled back to show the inside of the stable. There was a low bench for Mary to sit on and a real manger made of metal bars. It had a lot of straw on it and then a blanket for the baby to lie on.

Sarah quickly pulled out the pillow and took the Josh from Mrs Sinclair. She carried Josh, just how she had been shown, and put him in the manger. Josh lay there quietly.

The vicar read some more of the story and then the shepherds stood in front of the stable and the angel appeared. The angel had sparkly lights all over and a large glowing halo.

The shepherds walked around leading the lambs and then went to the stable. They held Tom up in front of Josh, who looked up at him and said "Gah!" Being a little tiny baby that is all he could say.

They went on with the practice until the three kings came. The first King came in and said he had come from far away to worship the baby Jesus. Then he went over to the manger where Josh was sleeping, and bowed. The King's crown fell off onto Josh who woke up and cried. The other kings helped put the crown back and Sarah picked up baby Josh and comforted him until he was quiet again.

Mrs Smith said, "Perhaps Mary should hold Jesus when the Kings come."

The Vicar said "Instead of bowing, the kings could all kneel to worship Jesus. Let's try that."

So the kings went out and did the scene again with Sarah sitting, holding Josh, and the kings kneeling in front of her and giving their presents which Sam took and looked after.

When the rehearsal was finished the Vicar said "All back here at two-thirty, please. We start at three."

Sarah and Sam changed into their ordinary clothes and helped their Dad give the sheep and lambs more feed and water. Then they went home and had lunch.

They were back well before half-past two and so were a lot of other people. Other families from the school were there, people from the town and the church, all waiting to see the play.

Tom and Tilly's Christmas Play

The children were petting the lambs and sheep, and the twins' Dad went to make sure they were all right.

Soon the children were dressed in their clothes with Sarah's pillow back as a baby bump. They looked a colourful crowd with their gowns and tea-towel head-dresses. Some of the parents took photos of them.

Sam tried pulling the donkey. "Look," he said, "It is really easy to lead now. I just have to pull."

"Pull it slowly though," said Sam's Dad. "We don't want Mary falling off!"

The Shepherds went and collected their lambs. The other children had to leave them and just play with the sheep, but Bud and Barb knew how to give them a good time. Some of the little tiny children could ride on them if their parents held them. Lots more people took photos.

Now people were beginning to sit down to watch the play. The adults sat on chairs at the back and children sat in the front on the grass. It was getting a bit windy but everyone could see the stage comfortably.

The Vicar welcomed everyone and said how well and hard the children had worked learning their lines. He then said a little prayer and they were almost ready to start the play.

Just then, Crash! Bang! Thunder and lightning started and rain began to fall.

"Oh, No!" Sarah said. "How can we have it in the rain?"

"Quick," said the Vicar "Everyone into the hall. Take your chairs. Can some of you help take the scenery into the hall"

Everyone ran and soon they were all seated in the hall. The scenery was in place. And they were all ready to start.

Tom and Tilly's Christmas Play

"What about the lambs?" Asked William, one of the shepherds, "Can we bring them in?"

"They are very small lambs," the Vicar said, "But if they make a mess you boys will have to clean it up!"

The play started. It was raining heavily outside so they all had to talk very loudly to make sure they were heard.

The play went well and the lambs were so good. Afterwards, they were taken back to their pen and given some extra hay.

After the play, there was a big tea in the back of the hall with doughnuts and lots of people came and said how well the children had done.

Sarah and Sam were pleased but they knew it was the lambs that had made the play such a success.